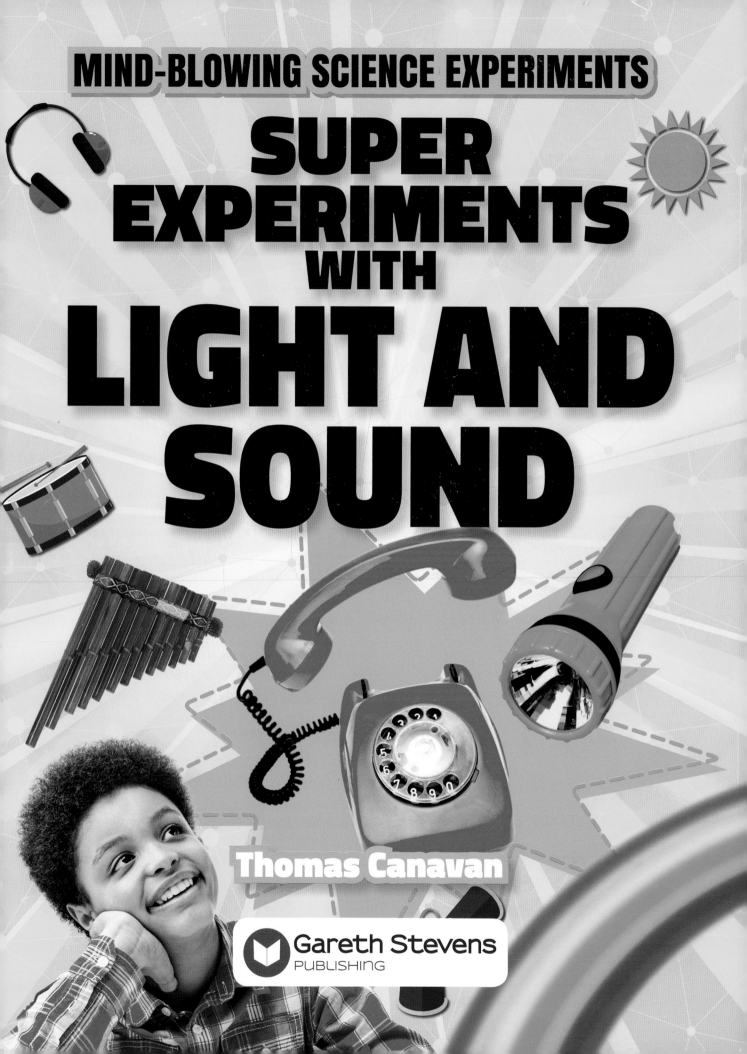

MIND-BLOWING SCIENCE EXPERIMENTS

SUPER EXPERIMENTS WITH LIGHT AND SOUND

Thomas Canavan

Gareth Stevens
PUBLISHING

Please visit our website, www.garethstevens.com.
For a free color catalog of all our high-quality books,
call toll free 1-800-542-2595 or fax 1-877-542-2596.

Cataloging-in-Publication Data
Names: Canavan, Thomas.
Title: Super experiments with light and sound / Thomas Canavan.
Description: New York : Gareth Stevens Publishing, 2018. | Series: Mind-blowing science experiments | Includes index.
Identifiers: ISBN 9781538207475 (pbk.) | ISBN 9781538207451 (library bound) | ISBN 9781538207338 (6 pack)
Subjects: LCSH: Light--Experiments--Juvenile literature. | Sound--Experiments--Juvenile literature.
Classification: LCC QC360.C317 2018 | DDC 535.078--dc23

Published in 2018 by
Gareth Stevens Publishing
111 East 14th Street, Suite 349
New York, NY 10003

Copyright © 2018 Arcturus Holdings Limited

Author: Thomas Canavan
Illustrator: Adam Linley
Experiments Coordinator: Anna Middleton
Designer: Elaine Wilkinson
Designer series edition: Emma Randall
Editors: Joe Harris, Rebecca Clunes, Frances Evans

All images courtesy of Shutterstock.

Printed in the United States of America
CPSIA compliance information: Batch CS17GS: For further information contact
Gareth Stevens, New York, New York at 1-800-542-2595.

Having Fun and Being Safe

Inside this book you'll find a whole range of exciting science experiments that can be performed safely at home. Nearly all the equipment you need will be found around your own house. Anything that you don't have at home should be available at a local store.

We have given some recommendations alongside the instructions to let you know when adult help might be needed. However, the degree of adult supervision will vary, depending on the age of the reader and the experiment. We would recommend close adult supervision for any experiment involving cooking equipment, sharp implements, electrical equipment, or batteries.

The author and publisher cannot take responsibility for any injury, damage, or mess that might occur as a result of attempting the experiments in this book. Always tell an adult before you perform any experiments, and follow the instructions carefully.

Contents

A note about measurements

Measurements are given in U.S. form with metric in parentheses. The metric conversion is rounded to make it easier to measure.

You're entering a world where things aren't quite what they seem. Did you ever think that you'd manage to slow the speed of light or make a dinner fork ring out like a gong? Prepare to be amazed!

Slowing the Speed of Light

Scientists tell us that the speed of light is as fast as anything can go—it's a speed limit for the whole universe! Nothing can go faster than the speed of light, but could you make light travel more slowly? Time to find out.

1
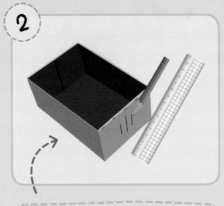

Measure the exact middle of one of the short ends of the shoe box and mark it with a vertical line.

2

Measure and mark two vertical lines, each about 1 inch (3 cm) long, on either side of the first mark. The parallel lines should each be about ¾ inch (2 cm) apart.

3
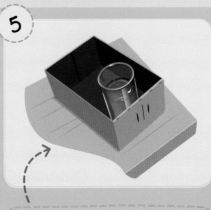

Rest the box on a flat surface, open side up. Ask an adult to use the scissors to cut along the two outside lines. This will create slits in the box.

4
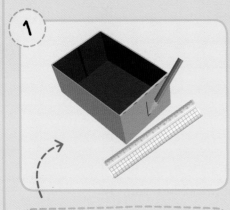

Darken the room and shine the flashlight through the slits. Observe how the light passes through the inside of the box.

5
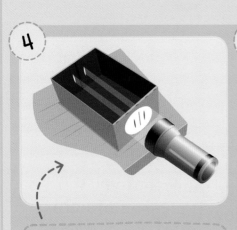

Fill the glass with water and place it inside the shoe box, just behind the two slits.

6
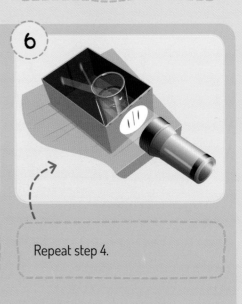

Repeat step 4.

HOW DOES IT WORK?

Light definitely has an upper speed limit, but there's no lower limit. This means light behaves differently as it passes through different substances. Passing through just air, as in step 4, it seems unaffected, which is why the bands of light remain **parallel**. But as light passes through water, it slows down and its rays bend. You can see how the light changes direction—a process called **refraction**—in the way the beams of light cross in step 6. The amount that light is refracted depends on an object's optical density.

WHAT HAPPENS IF...?

You can test the optical density of different substances by changing this experiment several times. First, you can try it with different liquids. For example, does the light behave differently as it passes through cooking oil? Or warmer water? What if the sides of the glass were thicker? Try to **predict** how the light will behave in these different circumstances.

TOP TIP!

Try moving the glass of water closer to, or further from, the slits to get the best image of the beams of light passing through.

REAL-LIFE SCIENCE

Lenses are curved pieces of a **transparent** substance, such as glass. The amount of glass along this curve determines how much the passing light is slowed and redirected. Convex lenses are thicker in the middle and focus light on a point. Concave lenses are thicker at the edges and send light out like a fan.

TOP TIP!

Make sure that the circle of light from the flashlight is wide enough to cover both slits completely.

sounding off

What do your school gym, musical recorders, and some careful footwork have to do with microwaves and radios? Quite a lot, in fact, as you'll see in this great experiment. You'll need to use a large empty room, which is why your school gym (or similar setting) is ideal.

YOU WILL NEED

- A large empty room (like a school gym)
- 2 chairs
- 2 recorders (musical instruments)
- 2 friends who can play the recorder
- Paper, cut into about 20 playing-card-sized pieces
- Pencils
- More friends to help you

1

Write "loud" on half of the papers and "soft" on the other half. Give your friends some of each type.

2

Set the chairs about five paces apart in the middle of the room.

3

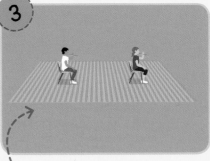

Have the "musician-scientists" sit in the chairs and get comfortable — they'll need to hold a note for a long time!

4

Ask each to play an identical note — for example, a B — and to hold it for as long as possible.

5

You and your friends should walk around the room, listening to how loud or quiet the music sounds. Everyone will have to stop each time the musicians pause to catch their breath.

6

Leave a paper marked "loud" on the floor in every spot the music sounds loud, and leave a "soft" piece of paper for the quiet spots.

HOW DOES IT WORK?

Sound, like other forms of **energy**, travels in waves. You can even imagine these waves being like those that crash on a beach. The high point of each wave is called a peak and the low point is a trough. A wave becomes stronger if the peak of a second wave meets the peak of the first wave.

A peak meeting a trough can cancel the strength of both waves. The same is true of sound waves, and your experiment shows where the peaks meet (loud, clear signal) and where there are "dead zones" (peak meeting trough), leading to less sound.

TOP TIP!

It's important that your musicians play the same note at the same time and volume.

WHAT HAPPENS IF...?

Does this demonstration work in larger settings? The answer is YES. Concertgoers would be angry if "dead zones" caused by wave interference silenced some of the music. Special equipment, which measures the motion of sound waves, helps architects and engineers design the best size and shape of concert halls and theaters to avoid creating any "dead zones."

REAL-LIFE SCIENCE

Sound isn't the only thing that travels in waves. The same is true of light, radio, and all sorts of **radiation**. Have you ever wondered why microwaves have rotating tables? That's to make sure that there are no "dead zones" of uncooked food where the waves cancel each other out.

Red Hot — or Not?

Artists refer to colors as "warm" or "cool." Is there a scientific explanation behind these descriptions? Imagine if you could measure the temperature of different colors. Well, you can—with this experiment. It's all about what makes up light.

YOU WILL NEED

- A **prism**
- Black tape
- Counter or table against a wall (must be near an outside window)
- Sheet of white paper
- Thermometer with liquid (not digital) display
- Pencil and paper
- Sticky tape

1

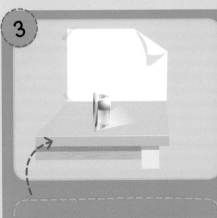

You want a clean, white wall for this experiment. If you don't have one, you should tape a piece of paper to the wall to create a white surface.

2

Cover the base (bulb) of the thermometer with black tape. This will help it absorb more heat, to create more dramatic results.

Whether you're using a prism, another tool, or just your eyes, never look directly into the Sun!

3

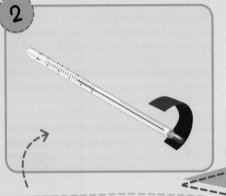

Rest your prism on the table or counter so that it's in the sunlight.

4

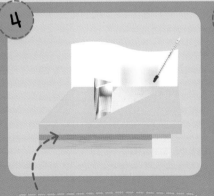

Lay the thermometer flat, jutting out from the wall, so that the bulb is in the blue section of the spectrum.

5

Wait a minute and then record the temperature.

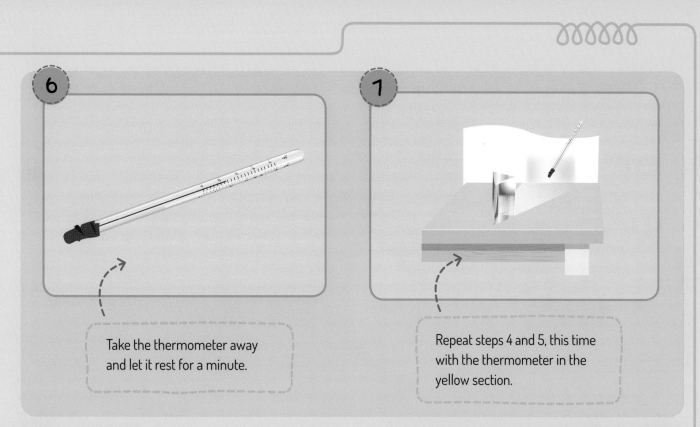

6

Take the thermometer away
and let it rest for a minute.

7

Repeat steps 4 and 5, this time
with the thermometer in the
yellow section.

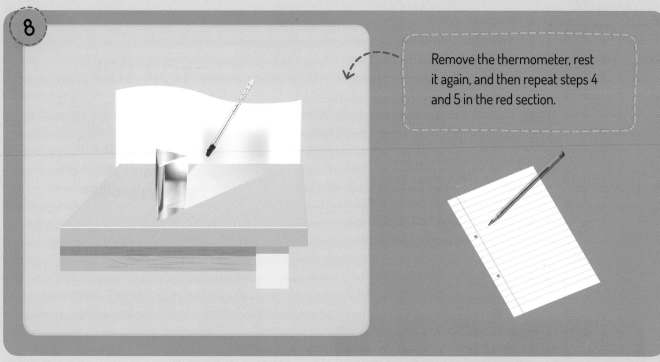

8

Remove the thermometer, rest
it again, and then repeat steps 4
and 5 in the red section.

TOP TIP!

You'll get the best results
on a sunny day when
the light is strongest.

Continued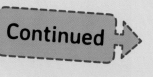

HOW DOES IT WORK?

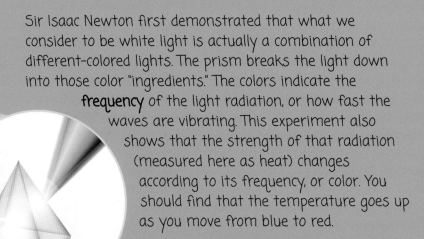

Sir Isaac Newton first demonstrated that what we consider to be white light is actually a combination of different-colored lights. The prism breaks the light down into those color "ingredients." The colors indicate the **frequency** of the light radiation, or how fast the waves are vibrating. This experiment also shows that the strength of that radiation (measured here as heat) changes according to its frequency, or color. You should find that the temperature goes up as you move from blue to red.

WHAT HAPPENS IF...?

Another great scientist, William Herschel, was the first to measure the temperature of the different-colored lights of the spectrum. He did something extra—which you can also try. You can take a fourth temperature reading, just as you did for the first three. This time, measure in what seems to be normal white just to the right of the red zone. Do you notice anything special?

TOP TIP!

The closer your prism is to the wall, the clearer the spectrum will appear—and you'll get better readings.

REAL-LIFE SCIENCE

Herschel's observation of warmer temperatures to the right of red was the first proof that there are forms of light that we can't see. He had discovered—and perhaps you've measured—infrared light. This and other forms of "invisible" light are vital in medicine and used in many everyday objects, such as remote controls.

Lasting Impression

You've probably heard the phrase "lasting impression" before. Normally, this is just a figure of speech that means something is very memorable. In this demonstration, you can create a *real* lasting impression! Plus, you'll learn about how our brains process what our eyes see.

YOU WILL NEED

- Thick cardboard
- Pencil
- Ruler
- Scissors
- Small flashlight
- Clear tape
- Room that will be dark if lights are off

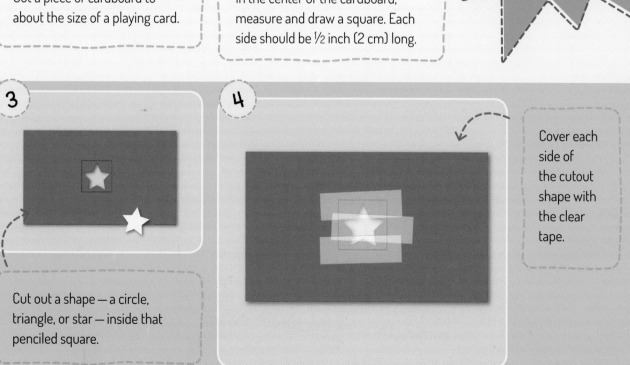

1
Cut a piece of cardboard to about the size of a playing card.

2
In the center of the cardboard, measure and draw a square. Each side should be ½ inch (2 cm) long.

Don't look at the light for too long! Make sure the light from the flashlight isn't too strong. If your eyes start to hurt, stop.

3
Cut out a shape — a circle, triangle, or star — inside that penciled square.

4
Cover each side of the cutout shape with the clear tape.

11

5

Turn off the lights.

6

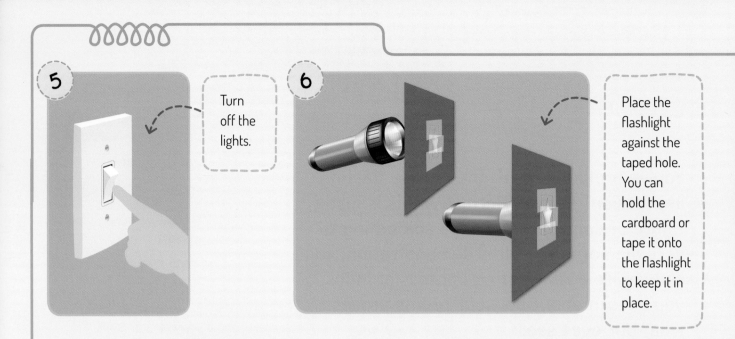

Place the flashlight against the taped hole. You can hold the cardboard or tape it onto the flashlight to keep it in place.

7

Hold the flashlight and cardboard in this position at arm's length and stare at the light for about 30 seconds.

8

Turn on the lights and gaze at a blank wall, blinking a little. You should see a dark image of the shape you were staring at in step 7.

TOP TIP!

Make sure that the piece of cardboard is big enough to block all of the light from the flashlight, except the light coming through the cutout shape.

HOW DOES IT WORK?

The retina is the area of your eye that is sensitive to light, and it sits at the back of your eye. Incoming light triggers chemical changes which the retina sends on to the brain. The part of the retina that receives a strong light signal (for example, from the bright shape) becomes less sensitive. When you look at the wall, that part of the retina doesn't react to the incoming light. The result? A lasting impression of "no light," or darkness. That negative image eventually fades after about 30 seconds, as the retina readjusts.

WHAT HAPPENS IF...?

Wonder whether it's your retina or your brain that's playing this trick on you? Try the experiment again, but close one eye as you look at the bright shape. Then close the other eye (the one that's just looked at the light) as you look at the wall. You won't see a "lasting impression" because that retina hadn't been affected.

REAL-LIFE SCIENCE

Scientists are fascinated by the way that human and animal eyes work. Experiments like this one can lead to more complicated medical studies, especially on how photoreceptors (light-sensitive cells in the retina) help us to distinguish colors and to see in the dark.

The "Nuttiest" Sound

Here's a simple experiment that manages to explain the nuts and bolts—or at least the nuts—of how sound is produced and heard. It might be the easiest experiment in this whole book, but it links to many other scientific examples.

1

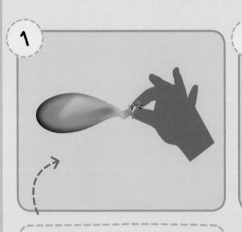

Carefully slip the nut into the balloon.

2

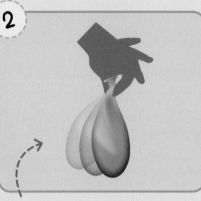

Hold the balloon by its narrow "lip" end and shake it lightly to make sure that the nut is all the way down.

3

Blow up the balloon and tie it shut.

4

Hold the balloon by the knot, with your hand pointing down.

5

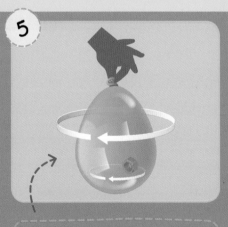

Swirl the balloon in a circular motion until the nut begins to race around the inside of the balloon.

6

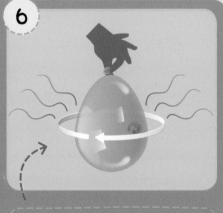

Listen to the weird, piercing sound that's produced!

HOW DOES IT WORK?

How does this freaky experiment work? First, centripetal **force** causes the nut to race around and around inside of the balloon. It pulls the nut inwards and stops it from flying straight off. As the nut speeds along, its six corners tap the inside of the balloon. Each tap creates a vibration that is transmitted through the air as a sound. The individual sounds are produced so quickly that they create a scary screaming noise.

TOP TIP!

You may find it easier to swirl the balloon if you make sure the knot is in the palm of your hand, with your hand pointing downwards.

REAL-LIFE SCIENCE

A satellite orbits the Earth using the same scientific force. Like the nut, it travels fast, and without the force of **gravity** pulling it in, it would fly off into outer space. The nut would also fly off its course if the balloon burst and it no longer pulled the nut inwards.

WHAT HAPPENS IF...?

One measure of sound is its frequency, or how often the waves of vibration are produced. Once you've got the hang of this balloon spinning, try getting the nut to travel faster or slower. Predict what you'll hear beforehand and then test your predictions by listening.

Seeing Sound

The world would be a pretty funny place if you could see sounds, wouldn't it? But is it such a crazy idea? After all, sounds are really vibrations that are picked up by our ears. So maybe there's a way of seeing those vibrations? Why not find out?

YOU WILL NEED

- Empty 2-liter plastic bottle
- Scissors
- Plastic grocery bag
- Rubber band
- Tea light
- Table
- Matches
- Ruler

1

5 cm

Ask an adult to cut around the bottle about 2 inches (5 cm) from the base.

2

Y

3 x Y

Cut a circle from the bag that's about three times bigger than the widest part of the bottle.

3

Lay that piece of plastic over the base of the bottle (the bit where you've just cut).

4

Stretch the rubber band over and around the base so that it holds the plastic firmly in place.

5

Tap the plastic lightly — you should hear a drumming sound.

6

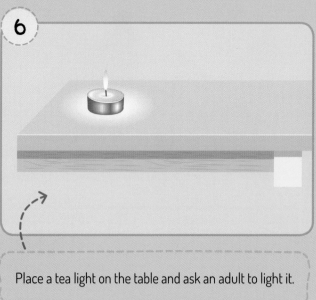

Place a tea light on the table and ask an adult to light it.

7

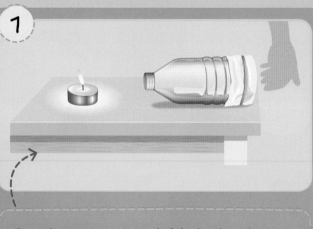

Point the narrow, open end of the bottle at the tea light and tap the drum on the other end.

8

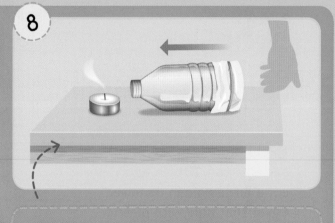

Move the bottle a little closer to the tea light if it doesn't blow out.

Ask an adult to cut the bottle and light the candle.

TOP TIP!

If the plastic hangs too loosely over the base of the bottle, either double-up the band to make it tighter or use a slightly smaller band.

Continued

HOW DOES IT WORK?

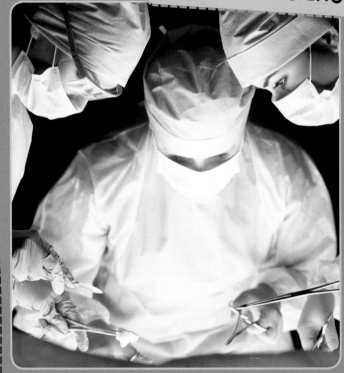

Sounds are vibrations, called sound waves, that are sent through the air. Our ears pick up these vibrations, process them, and send them to our brains electrically. This is where we heard them as sounds.

In the ocean, each incoming wave pushes you towards shore. The sound waves you produced by tapping on the plastic also had some "push." In this case, that force was enough to cause the moving air to blow out the candle.

WHAT HAPPENS IF...?

You can try this same experiment on a larger scale. See if you can find an old (but clean!) plastic garbage can. Ask an adult to cut a large hole in its base. Cover that hole with plastic and rope, just like you did earlier with plastic and rubber bands. Aim the other end at the candle. You should be able to extinguish the flame from much further away!

REAL-LIFE SCIENCE

Scientists are constantly finding new uses for sound waves and the force that they produce. By focusing the waves in a particular direction, they can cause objects to levitate (float) or move along a surface. Sound waves may soon even provide a way of performing surgery without cutting people open.

Frozen Lantern

YOU WILL NEED

- An LED
- 2 lengths of thin, insulated copper wire about 16 inches (40 cm) long
- Balloon
- 12-inch (30 cm) length of string or a freezer bag clip
- Electrical tape
- Water
- Freezer
- 1.5 volt battery (AA is the best size)
- A friend

A scientific experiment begins with a hypothesis, or a prediction about what will happen. What do you think will happen to light as it shines through ice? See if your hypothesis is right when you try out this experiment!

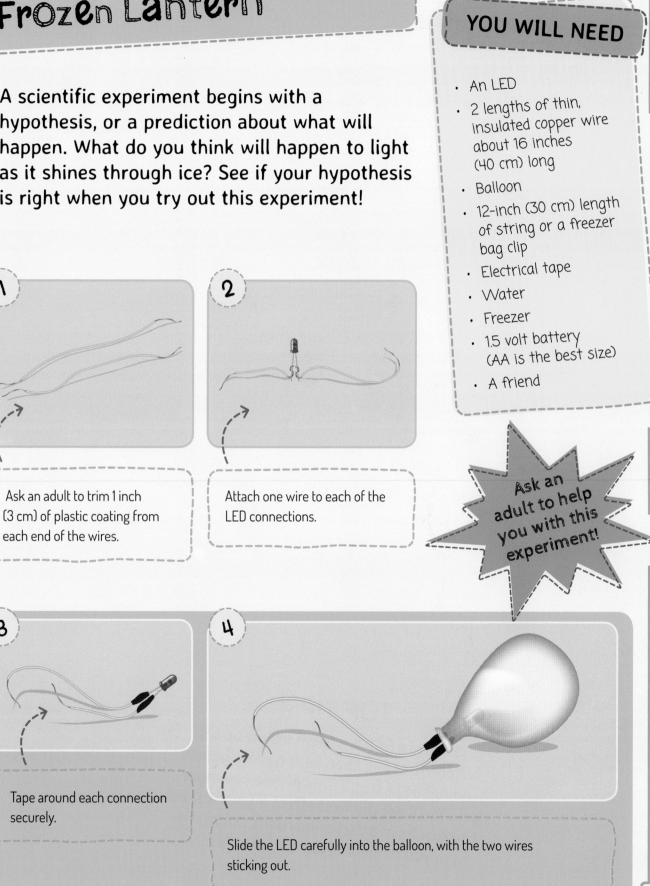

1 Ask an adult to trim 1 inch (3 cm) of plastic coating from each end of the wires.

2 Attach one wire to each of the LED connections.

Ask an adult to help you with this experiment!

3 Tape around each connection securely.

4 Slide the LED carefully into the balloon, with the two wires sticking out.

19

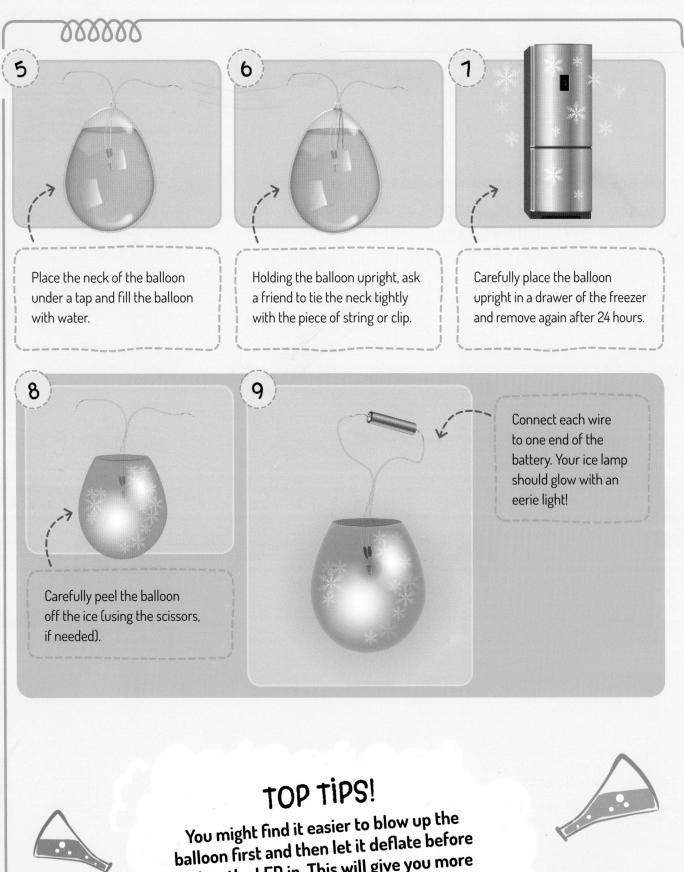

5 Place the neck of the balloon under a tap and fill the balloon with water.

6 Holding the balloon upright, ask a friend to tie the neck tightly with the piece of string or clip.

7 Carefully place the balloon upright in a drawer of the freezer and remove again after 24 hours.

8 Carefully peel the balloon off the ice (using the scissors, if needed).

9 Connect each wire to one end of the battery. Your ice lamp should glow with an eerie light!

TOP TiPS!

You might find it easier to blow up the balloon first and then let it deflate before sliding the LED in. This will give you more slack. You'll get the best effect if you can test the results in a darkened room, but make sure you're holding the ice lamp firmly.

HOW DOES IT WORK?

Hooking up the LED to the battery is a good demonstration of an electrical flow. But why is the result so... spooky? After all, water is clear, so you'd expect to be able to look through 4 inches (10 cm) or so of ice to have a clear view of the LED.

Ice is made up of crystals that reflect light in every direction. This is called a diffuse reflection. Tiny bubbles and particles locked inside the ice also contribute to this blurred reflection.

WHAT HAPPENS IF...?

What would happen if you used distilled or purified water to make the ice? Both of these involve cleaning and filtering out impurities.

REAL-LIFE SCIENCE

We come across diffused, or scattered, light constantly in nature. Just look up. A clear sky looks blue because sunlight hits particles of nitrogen and oxygen in the atmosphere, causing blue light to scatter more than other colors. And why are most clouds white? Well, they're made of ice crystals, which scatter light just like your lantern!

Hold the Line, Please

You've seen landline phones, but did you know there's another kind of "line" you can use to communicate with your friends? Follow these steps to engineer your own basic telephone!

YOU WILL NEED

- 2 plastic cups
- String that is about 33 feet (10 m) long
- Paper clips
- Sharp pencil

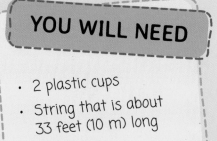

1

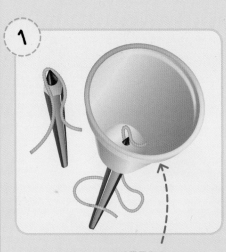

Pinch one end of the string to the tip of the pencil and gently poke it through the bottom of the cup, from the outside in.

2

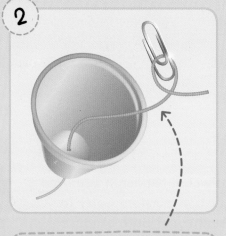

Pull the string through enough to tie it to the end of a paper clip.

3

Feed the other end of the string into the other cup and also tie it to a paper clip.

4

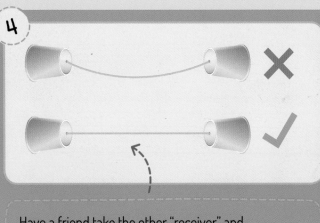

Have a friend take the other "receiver" and walk away until the string stops drooping and seems tight.

5

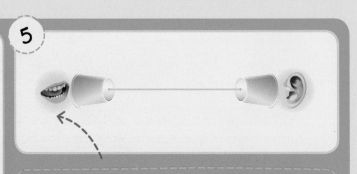

Speak into one end and find out if your friend can hear you. Try feeding the line through the gap of an open door or behind curtains so one of you can remain hidden.

22

HOW DOES IT WORK?

The word telephone comes from two Greek words. "Tele" means "far," and "phone" means "sound," or "voice." When put together, these words roughly mean "distant voice." Your homemade telephone lets you hear just that!

Your telephone uses some of the same principles as a landline telephone. When you speak, the string begins to vibrate, sending those vibrations down the line. The cup at the other end amplifies (increases) the sounds those vibrations make, so the other person can hear you. A landline telephone also receives and plays back vibrations, but uses electricity to send them over much greater distances.

WHAT HAPPENS IF...?

This experiment is all about how sound behaves because it is a type of vibration. Try to see which type of sound vibrations travel best along your "phone line." Does it work better if you speak high (creating lots of vibrations) or low (creating fewer vibrations)?

REAL-LIFE SCIENCE

This experiment works best with a short, taut string. If you try doing this experiment with a much longer piece of string, you'll notice that the other person's voice becomes harder to hear. That's because some of the vibration energy has been lost along the way, so the sound waves become weaker. Real telephone signals also lose energy over distances. That's why telephone signal boosters are needed.

What happens to the sound if the string is loose?

The Wrong Balloon

Have you ever seen a big balloon with a smaller balloon inside it? It's a pretty cool trick, but that's just the beginning of this experiment! If you use a magnifying glass, you can focus the sunlight and pop just the inner balloon! Can science explain that one, please?

1

Blow up the clear balloon and pinch it shut.

2

Feed the black balloon into the clear balloon, leaving some of the black balloon sticking out of the mouth of the other balloon.

3

Blow up the black balloon about halfway and tie it shut.

4

Push the black balloon inside and tie the clear balloon shut. You now have two balloons, one inside the other.

5

Hold the magnifying glass so that it shines the sunlight on the pair of balloons.

6

Move the magnifying glass until it focuses the beam on the black balloon. It will pop in a few seconds!

HOW DOES IT WORK?

Darker-colored objects absorb more energy (including heat) from the light than lighter objects. This is why sunlight passes through the clear balloon without bursting it. When it reaches the inner balloon, the concentrated light (and heat) from the magnifying glass quickly heats the balloon until it pops. This also happens with other forms of radiation. X-rays pass through skin and muscle but are absorbed by bones and teeth, which is why they show up so clearly on X-ray photographs.

REAL-LIFE SCIENCE

People in very hot countries often dress in light-colored clothing. That's because light colors don't absorb as much heat as darker clothing would.

TOP TIPS!

Never look directly at the Sun.

Don't let the magnifying glass focus its light on anything delicate or valuable.

WHAT HAPPENS IF...?

Try doing the experiment in reverse, with the clear balloon blown up inside the black one. Is it still the inside balloon that pops? Why is that?

The CD Rainbow

Now you know that white light is actually a combination of all the colors. You also know that you can "build" white by adding those colors together. Here's a chance to do the opposite—split white light apart to reveal its hidden color ingredients!

YOU WILL NEED

- CD
- Flashlight
- Sunny day

1

If it's a sunny day, stand by a window and hold the CD in front of you with the shiny side facing up. Hold the CD almost flat and observe the light it reflects.

2

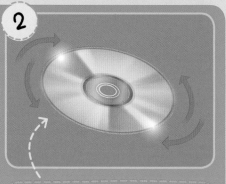

Gently tilt the CD left, right, forward, and backward until you see a band of different colors.

3

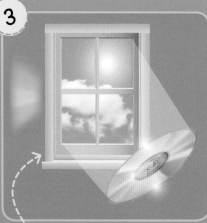

Now see if you can project the band of colors onto a wall or blank surface near the window.

4

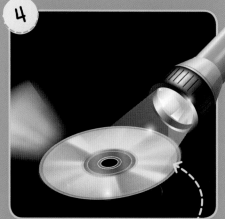

Turn the lights off and find a dark part of the room. Shine the flashlight onto the shiny side of the CD.

5

Move the flashlight and the CD until you see the rainbow again. By angling the flashlight and the CD, you're reflecting light from the different ridges and sending out different reflected colors.

HOW DOES IT WORK?

The "white light" we see from the Sun or a flashlight is actually a combination of all the colors. Light travels in waves, a bit like waves approaching a beach. Sometimes ocean waves "team up" and become bigger, and sometimes they crash into each other and cancel each other out.

The shiny side of the CD is actually made of tiny ridges. Light waves reflect from these ridges in different angles, some "teaming up" and others canceling out. Those changes to the waves upset the neat balance of colors. Instead, we see some of them more clearly.

WHAT HAPPENS IF...?

Now flip the CD over and try the same things with the shiny side down. Do you think that you'll see the rainbow of colors this time? Were your predictions right?

TOP TIPS!

You could use a DVD instead of a CD!

REAL-LIFE SCIENCE

When you see a rainbow, you're looking at a natural version of the experiment you just did. Each raindrop in the sky refracts the white light into "all the colors of the rainbow," or the spectrum. But those colors are reflected off at different angles, so we see only one of the colors from each raindrop. And with so many raindrops up there, every color gets a chance to be seen!

Dinner Gongs

Have you ever seen a dinner gong? Some are as big as garbage can lids! Imagine if you could trick your ears into hearing a sound as loud as a giant gong using only forks, spoons, and butter knives. Maybe you can!

YOU WILL NEED

- Metal butter knife, fork, and spoon
- Thread or thin string
- Scissors
- Ruler

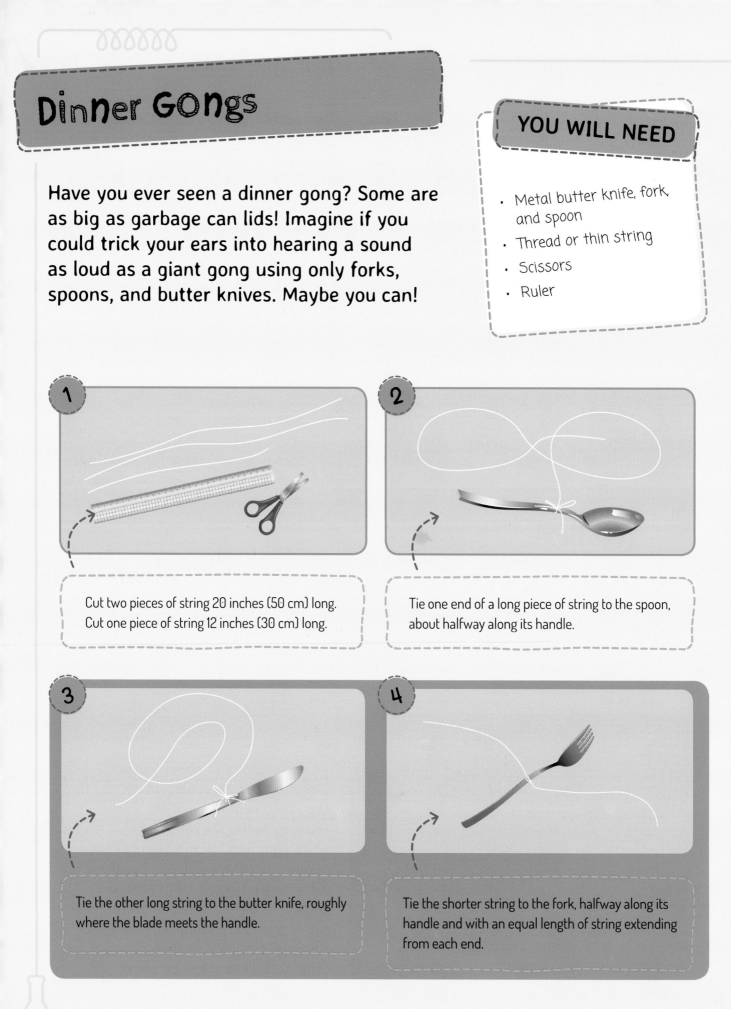

1 Cut two pieces of string 20 inches (50 cm) long. Cut one piece of string 12 inches (30 cm) long.

2 Tie one end of a long piece of string to the spoon, about halfway along its handle.

3 Tie the other long string to the butter knife, roughly where the blade meets the handle.

4 Tie the shorter string to the fork, halfway along its handle and with an equal length of string extending from each end.

5

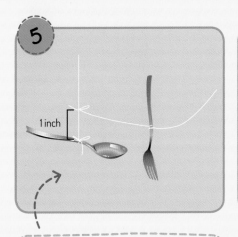

1 inch

Tie one of the free ends of the short string to the spoon's string. Tie the knot about 1 inch (3 cm) up from the spoon.

6

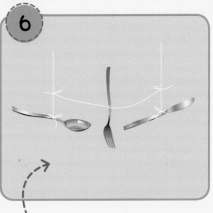

Repeat step 5 with the other free end of the short string. Tie it 1 inch (3 cm) up from the butter knife.

7

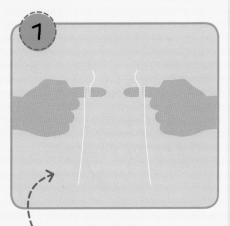

Wrap the free end of each long string around an index finger and press those fingertips to your ears. The spoon, knife, and fork will be dangling below your head. Bend forward slightly.

8

Shake your head back and forth two or three times.

9

You should hear a clear, bell-like sound.

TOP TiP!

You might need to adjust the strings to make sure the three pieces of cutlery hang at roughly the same distance below your head.

Continued

HOW DOES IT WORK?

Don't forget that what you hear as sound is actually a series of vibrations, which tiny bones in your ears detect. They then transform the vibrations into a series of electrical signals that get sent to the brain. We normally pick up vibrations that have traveled through the air, but they can also travel through other substances. In this case, vibrations travel along a string and your fingers to your ears. Those vibrations have less chance to disperse and weaken (compared to traveling through the air), so you can hear the sounds more clearly. That's why three little pieces of cutlery can sound like a giant gong!

TOP TIP!

You only need to shake your head gently to get the best sound. If you swing too much, the utensils will swing past each other.

WHAT HAPPENS IF...?

You can combine this experiment with the telephone you made on pages 22–23 for some secret-agent action! Test how sound travels through other substances. Try using homemade phones underwater—with adult supervision, of course! Call out to your friend using the phone while you're both underwater. What do you hear?

REAL-LIFE SCIENCE

You can hear the different ways air can **conduct** sound. Blow up a balloon and hold it next to your ear. Listen to ordinary sounds, and they'll all become louder. That's because blowing up the balloon crowded the air **molecules** in the balloon together more tightly, which made them conduct sounds better.

Glossary

conduct To transmit heat or electricity.

energy The power or ability to do work such as moving. Energy can be transferred from one object to another, but it cannot be destroyed.

force The strength of a particular energy at work.

frequency How often something occurs.

gravity The force that causes all objects to be attracted to each other.

molecule The smallest unit of a substance, such as oxygen, that has all the properties of that substance.

optical density How light passes through a material.

parallel Describing lines that are the same distance apart at all points.

predict To say what will happen in the future or as a result of an action.

prism A clear, solid object that refracts light as it passes through so that it is broken up into the colors of the rainbow.

radiation Waves of energy sent out by sources of light or heat.

refract To cause waves (of light, heat or sound) to bend as they pass through a different material.

transparent A material that allows light to pass through, and objects can be clearly seen on the other side.

Further Information

Books to read

100 Steps for Science: Why it works and how it happened by Lisa Jane Gillespie and Yukai Du (Wide Eyed Editions, 2017)

Experiments with Sound and Light by Chris Oxlade (PowerKids Press, 2015)

Mind Webs: Light and Sound by Anna Claybourne (Wayland, 2015)

Websites

https://www.education.com/activity/light+and+sound/
Explore more with light and sound experiments at this awesome site!

https://www.stevespanglerscience.com/lab/categories/experiments/light–and–sound/
Find more fantastic projects with light and sound here!

https://www.exploratorium.edu/snacks/subject/light
This fun website is full of even more light and sound experiments to try!

Index